My World of Geography

MOUNTAINS

Angela Royston

Heinemann
LIBRARY

Young Explorer

www.heinemann.co.uk/library

Visit our website to find out more information about **Heinemann Library** books.

To order:

☎ Phone 44 (0) 1865 888066

🖹 Send a fax to 44 (0) 1865 314091

🖥 Visit the Heinemann Bookshop at www.heinemann.co.uk/library to browse our catalogue and order online.

First published in Great Britain by Heinemann Library, Halley Court, Jordan Hill, Oxford OX2 8EJ, part of Harcourt Education.
Heinemann is a registered trademark of Harcourt Education Ltd.

Editorial: Andrew Farrow and Dan Nunn
Design: Ron Kamen and Celia Jones
Illustrations: Barry Atkinson (p. 8, p. 17), Jo Brooker (p. 15), Jeff Edwards (p. 5, pp. 28–9)
Picture Research: Rebecca Sodergren, Melissa Allison and Debra Weatherley
Production: Duncan Gilbert

Originated by Ambassador Litho Ltd
Printed and bound in Hong Kong and China by South China Printing Co Ltd

The paper used to print this book comes from sustainable resources.

ISBN 0 431 11790 X
08 07 06 05 04
10 9 8 7 6 5 4 3 2 1

British Library Cataloguing in Publication Data

Royston, Angela
  Mountains. – (My world of geography)
  1. Mountains – Juvenile literature
  I. Title
  551.4'32

A full catalogue record for this book is available from the British Library.

Acknowledgements

The Publishers would like to thank the following for permission to reproduce photographs:

Alamy Images pp. **10** (Douglas Peebles), **20** (Imagestate/S. Barnett), **21** (Phototake Inc./Peter Treiber), **26** (Gallen Rowell); Bruce Coleman p. **27**; Corbis pp. **4**, **18** (Robert Essel NYC), **19** (Ray Juno), **24**; Getty Images pp. **7** (Digital Vision), **25** (Photodisc); Harcourt Education Ltd p. **11** (Tudor Photography); John Cleare Mountain Picture Library pp. **14**, **16**; NASA p. **6**; Nature Picture Library p. **12**; Robert Harding Picture Library p. **22**; Science Photo Library pp. **9** (Simon Fraser), **13** (Bernhard Edmaier).

Map on page 23 reproduced by permission of Ordnance Survey on behalf of the Controller of Her Majesty's Stationary Office, © Crown Copyright 100000230. Cover photograph reproduced with permission of Getty Images/Stone.

Every effort has been made to contact copyright holders of any material reproduced in this book. Any omissions will be rectified in subsequent printings if notice is given to the Publishers.

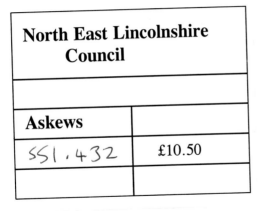

Contents

Some words are shown in bold, **like this**. You can find out what they mean by looking in the Glossary.

 Find out more about mountains at
www.heinemannexplore.co.uk

What is a mountain?

A mountain is a rocky piece of land that is much higher than the land around it. The top of a mountain is called the **summit**.

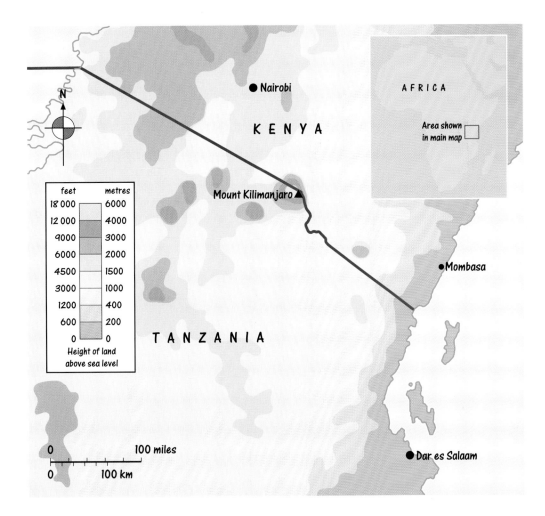

This map shows Mount Kilimanjaro in Africa. The mountain is shown by a black triangle. The height of the land is shown in different colours. The highest land is coloured light purple.

Mountain ranges

Most mountains are part of a mountain **range**. A range is a long chain of mountains that lie close together. Some mountain ranges stretch for thousands of kilometres.

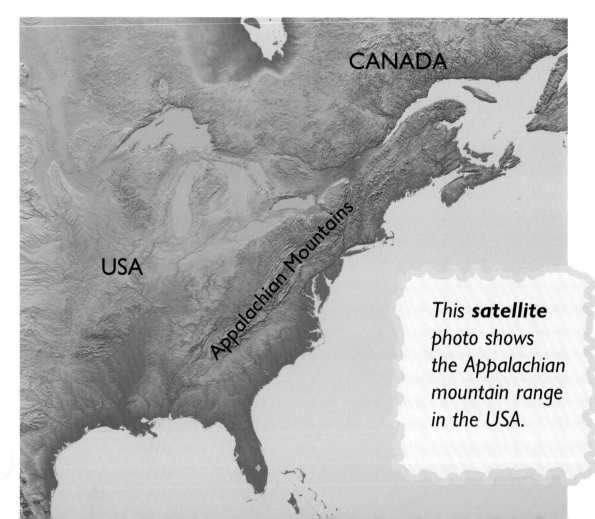

CANADA

USA

Appalachian Mountains

*This **satellite** photo shows the Appalachian mountain range in the USA.*

mountain

foothill

The mountains in the middle of a range are usually the highest. The hills around the edge are lower. They are called **foothills**.

Measuring mountains

In this diagram, mountains 1, 2 and 3 are all the same height. This is because mountains are always measured from their top to sea level.

❶ ❷ ❸

sea level

The height of a mountain is measured from its top to **sea level**. This way of measuring mountains is used all over the world.

People use many special **instruments** to measure the height of mountains. Sometimes the instruments are carried on an aeroplane or a **satellite**.

This climber is measuring the height of a mountain.

How mountains form

Most mountains form very slowly over millions of years. Huge forces from deep inside the Earth move parts of the land. Some of the land rises slowly.

These mountains are in Alaska, in North America. They are getting a tiny bit higher every year.

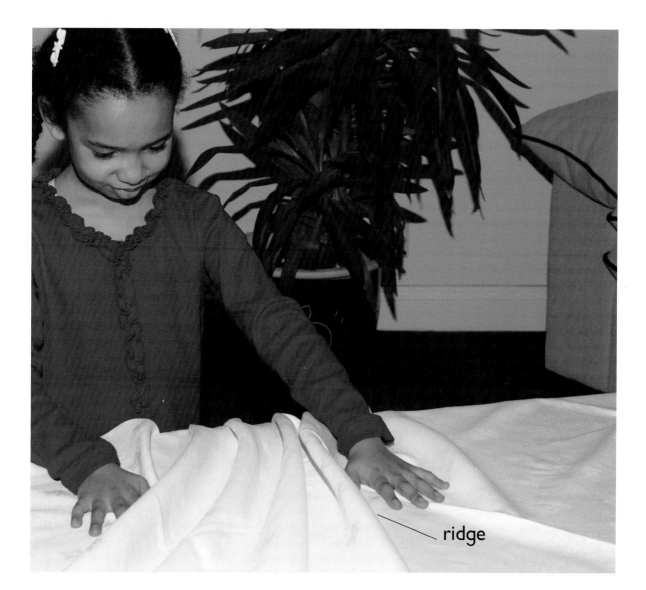

ridge

You can see the way some mountains are made by pushing a tablecloth on a smooth table. The cloth forms a ridge when it is pushed.

Volcanoes

Many mountains are made by **volcanoes**. When a volcano **erupts**, hot, runny rock called **lava** spills out from deep inside the Earth. The new rock cools and becomes hard.

lava

volcano

Each time a volcano erupts, new rock piles up higher and higher. Some volcanoes are still erupting. Some volcanoes stopped erupting long ago.

This volcano is on the island of Lanzarote. It stopped erupting many years ago.

Wearing down rocks

Mountains do not stay the same. The weather slowly wears them down. Wind, sunshine, rain and snow break up the rocks that form the mountain.

mountain top

Sometimes a whole cliff breaks up and falls down the mountainside!

rocky slope

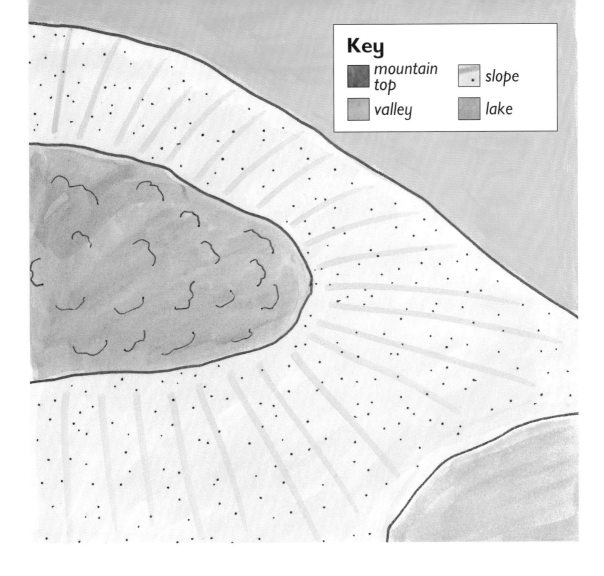

This map shows the same mountain as the photo on page 14. Some of the **cliff** has fallen down to form a rocky slope. You could draw a diagram like this.

Mountain weather

The weather becomes colder as you go up a mountain. The tops of the highest mountains are so cold they are always covered by snow.

This **mountaineer** is dressed in very warm clothes because the weather is so cold.

lots of rain

mountains

dry land or desert

The type of weather on one side of a mountain **range** is often different from the other side. On one side of the range it may be very wet, but on the other side there may be a **desert**.

Farming

People use the warm lower slopes of a mountain to farm. Farmers shape the sides of the mountain into flat areas called **terraces**. It is easier to grow **crops** on flat areas of land.

Terraces are like huge steps cut into the sides of the mountain.

The higher slopes on a mountain are often grassy. In summer, farmers take their cattle, sheep and goats up to the higher slopes to feed on the grass.

Mining

Some rocks contain valuable metals. Rocks in the Andes Mountains in South America contain copper, tin, gold and silver.

This rock has gold in it.

People dig rocks out of **mines**. They separate metal from the rocks. The rocks and metal are carried down the mountainside in trucks.

This man is mining gold in a gold mine.

Finding your way

It is fun to walk or climb in the mountains. Sometimes you can follow a path. A map and a **compass** can help you find your way.

This map shows an area of Wales, in the UK. It might be used by people out walking, so they don't get lost.

On this map the dotted lines are paths. The yellow lines are roads. Blue lines are streams and rivers. The brown loopy lines are **contour** lines. Contour lines show how steep and high up the places on the map are.

Enjoying mountains

Mountains are wild and beautiful places. Many people like to climb right to the top of mountains and enjoy the views.

Some people use mountain slopes for skiing on snow. A ski lift carries them to the top of the ski run. Then they push themselves off and ski back down the slope.

Protecting mountains

All mountains wear down slowly over time, but some mountains are being worn down too quickly. This is because so many people climb them that the paths become damaged.

This bear is catching a salmon in a national park in Alaska.

Many mountains are turned into **national parks**. This means that the animals that live there are protected. **Mines** cannot be dug in a national park.

Mountains of the world

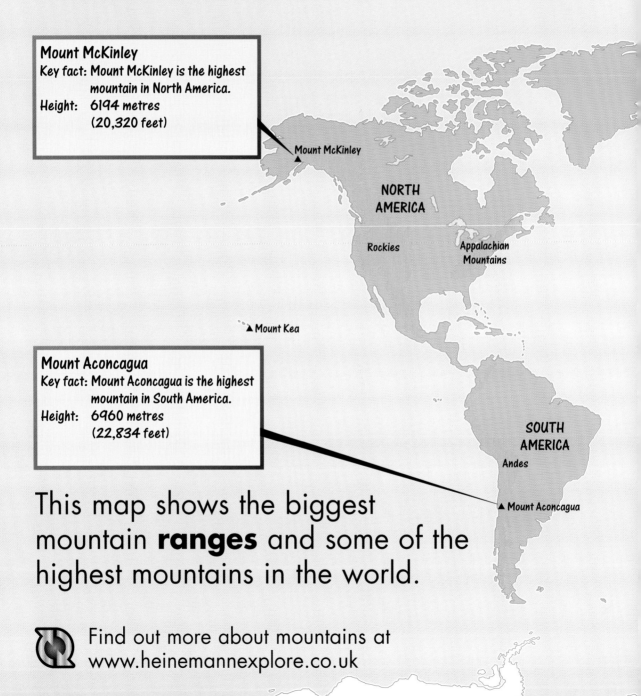

Mount McKinley

Key fact: Mount McKinley is the highest
mountain in North America.

Height: 6194 metres
(20,320 feet)

Mount Aconcagua

Key fact: Mount Aconcagua is the highest
mountain in South America.

Height: 6960 metres
(22,834 feet)

Mount McKinley

NORTH
AMERICA

Rockies

Appalachian
Mountains

▲ Mount Kea

SOUTH
AMERICA

Andes

▲ Mount Aconcagua

This map shows the biggest
mountain **ranges** and some of the
highest mountains in the world.

Find out more about mountains at
www.heinemannexplore.co.uk

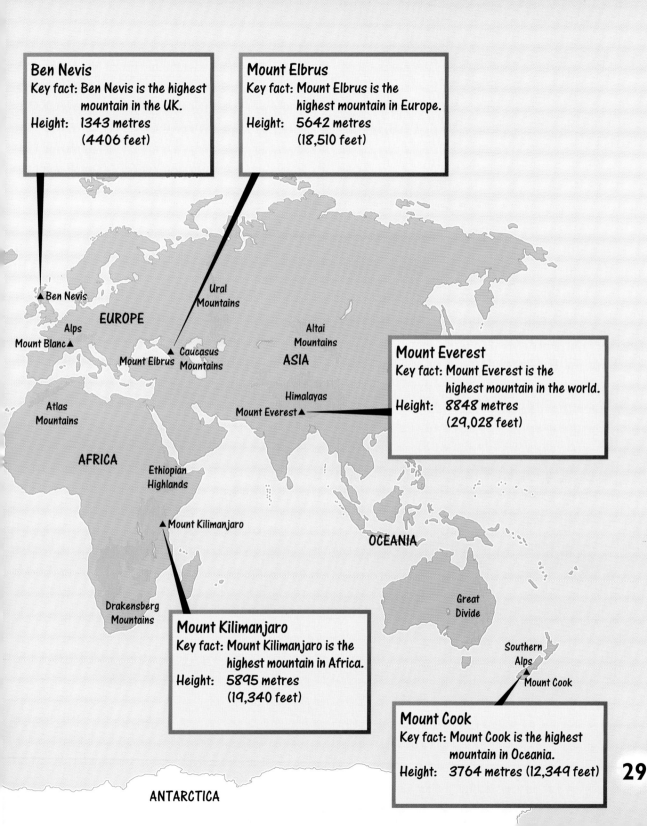

Ben Nevis
Key fact: Ben Nevis is the highest
mountain in the UK.
Height: 1343 metres
          (4406 feet)

Mount Elbrus
Key fact: Mount Elbrus is the
          highest mountain in Europe.
Height: 5642 metres
          (18,510 feet)

Mount Everest
Key fact: Mount Everest is the
          highest mountain in the world.
Height: 8848 metres
          (29,028 feet)

Mount Kilimanjaro
Key fact: Mount Kilimanjaro is the
          highest mountain in Africa.
Height: 5895 metres
          (19,340 feet)

Mount Cook
Key fact: Mount Cook is the highest
          mountain in Oceania.
Height: 3764 metres (12,349 feet)

▲ Ben Nevis

Ural
Mountains

EUROPE

Alps

Mount Blanc ▲

Mount Elbrus ▲

▲ Caucasus
Mountains

Altai
Mountains

ASIA

Atlas
Mountains

AFRICA

Ethiopian
Highlands

Himalayas
Mount Everest ▲

▲ Mount Kilimanjaro

OCEANIA

Great
Divide

Drakensberg
Mountains

Southern
Alps

▲ Mount Cook

29

ANTARCTICA

Glossary

cliff very steep slope

compass an instrument that shows the direction of north

contour a line on a map that shows how high somewhere is

crops plants grown for food

desert an area of very dry land, where there is not much rain

erupt burst out

foothill hill on the edge of a mountain range

instrument machine that helps you do something

lava hot, runny rock that erupts from a volcano

mine hole dug in the ground to get something valuable, such as metals or coal

mountaineer someone who climbs mountains

national park large area of countryside that is protected so people can enjoy its beauty

range several mountains grouped together

satellite object put into space that can take photographs or send TV signals, for example

sea level the height of the surface of the sea

summit the top of a mountain

terrace flat strip of land dug into the side of a mountain

volcano a place where lava escapes through a hole in the ground

Find out more

Further reading

Geography First: Mountains by Celia Tidmarsh (Hodder Wayland, 2004)

Geography First: Volcanoes by Chris Turbin (Hodder Wayland, 2004)

Eye Wonder: Volcano (Dorling Kindersley, 2003)

Geography Starts Here: Maps and Symbols by Angela Royston (Hodder Wayland, 2001)

Useful Websites

http://volcano.und.nodak.edu/vwdocs/kids/kids.html – site for young readers that contains stories, activities and games.

www.cadburylearningzone.co.uk/environment/gallery/galleryframe.htm – click on the bottom (brown) Yowie to get information about the Cairngorm mountains in Scotland and the threats to the environment.

Disclaimer

All the Internet addresses (URLs) given in this book were valid at the time of going to press. However, due to the dynamic nature of the Internet, some addresses may have changed, or sites may have changed or ceased to exist since publication. While the author and the Publishers regret any inconvenience this may cause readers, no responsibility for any such changes can be accepted by either the author or the Publishers.

Index

Titles in the *My World of Geography* series include:

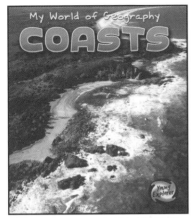

Hardback   0 431 11802 7

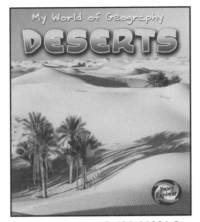

Hardback   0 431 11801 9

Hardback   0 431 11792 6

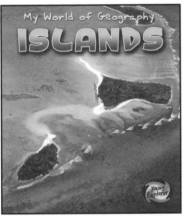

Hardback   0 431 11800 0

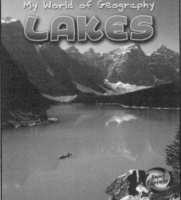

Hardback   0 431 11791 8

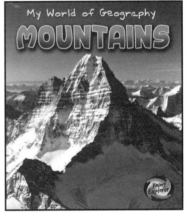

Hardback   0 431 11790 X

Hardback   0 431 11799 3

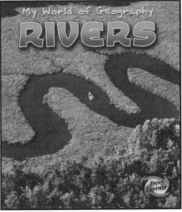

Hardback   0 431 11789 6

Find out about the other titles in this series on our website www.heinemann.co.uk/library